C000072349

GLADNESS AND GENEROSITY

GROUP STUDIES

LEADER'S GUIDE

Edited by
ANDREW ROBERTS

The Bible Reading Fellowship
15 The Chambers, Vineyard
Abingdon OX14 3FE
brf.org.uk

The Bible Reading Fellowship (BRF) is a Registered Charity (233280)

ISBN 978 0 85746 857 4
First published 2020
10 9 8 7 6 5 4 3 2 1 0
All rights reserved

Acknowledgements
Scripture quotations marked NRSV are taken from The New Revised Standard Version
of the Bible, Anglicised edition, copyright © 1989, 1995 by the Division of Christian
Education of the National Council of the Churches of Christ in the United States of
America. Used by permission. All rights reserved.

Scripture quotations marked NIV are taken from The Holy Bible, New International
Version (Anglicised edition) copyright © 1979, 1984, 2011 by Biblica. Used by
permission of Hodder & Stoughton Publishers, a Hachette UK company. All rights
reserved. 'NIV' is a registered trademark of Biblica. UK trademark number 1448790.

Every effort has been made to trace and contact copyright owners for material used
in this resource. We apologise for any inadvertent omissions or errors, and would
ask those concerned to contact us so that full acknowledgement can be made in
the future.

A catalogue record for this book is available from the British Library

Printed and bound in the UK by Zenith Media NP4 0DQ

Contents

About the writers

About the writers

Steve Aisthorpe is the Church of Scotland's mission development worker for the Highlands and Islands. He was previously executive director of the International Nepal Fellowship and is the author of *The Invisible Church* (SAP, 2016). He loves being outdoors, whatever the weather, and is an enthusiastic coach and retreat leader.

Jo Swinney is an author, speaker and director of communications for CPO. She has written six books, most recently *Home: The quest to belong* (Hodder, 2017). She has an MA in theology from Regent College, Vancouver, and loves writing about the Bible. She lives with her family in Bath and blogs at joswinney.com.

David Spriggs is a Baptist minister who has also served with the Evangelical Alliance and Bible Society. He has written several books and until recently was commissioning editor for BRF's *Guidelines* Bible reading notes. In 'retirement', he is the minister of a church in Leicester.

David Gilmore is a husband, father and ordained elder of the United Methodist Church who serves as director of congregational development and revitalisation for the New York Conference. He is responsible for planting new churches; identifying, equipping and empowering emerging leaders; and supporting and nurturing the creation of new ministries.

Introduction

Introduction

> They devoted themselves to the apostles' teaching and fellowship, to the breaking of bread and the prayers. Awe came upon everyone, because many wonders and signs were being done by the apostles. All who believed were together and had all things in common; they would sell their possessions and goods and distribute the proceeds to all, as any had need. Day by day, as they spent much time together in the temple, they broke bread at home and ate their food with glad and generous hearts, praising God and having the goodwill of all the people. And day by day the Lord added to their number those who were being saved.
>
> ACTS 2:42–47 (NRSV)

Holy Habits is a way of life to be lived by disciples of Jesus individually and collectively. As Alison Morgan points out in the subtitle of her book *Following Jesus*, the plural of disciple is church. When Jesus calls us to follow, he gifts us others to journey with us, just as he gifted his first disciples – others who will help to teach us and who will learn from us; others who will pray with us and check how we are; others who will watch over us in love and keep us accountable in our discipleship. In the light of this, these Group Studies and the complementary daily Bible Reflections have been written for both group and personal usage. In this booklet, you will find material to help you as a church or a small group reflect together on the particular holy habit being explored.

The authors (who also wrote the complementary Holy Habits Bible Reflections; see page 62) have formed questions for reflection and discussion. Each author has selected two of the readings from the ten they wrote about and provided six questions on each for discussion. Some have a more personal focus, while others relate more to the church or group as whole. With questions of a more personal nature, you may wish to invite people to discuss these in the confidence of pairs and then make time for anyone to share a response with the whole group if they would like to. This approach can also be a good way of making sure everyone has a chance to share if your group has newcomers or people who are shy or dominant.

You will then find a series of take-home questions about the habit. These have been collated from questions submitted by the authors, which mean they vary in style, tone and focus. As such, you may find some more helpful than others, so feel free to add or amend questions. As you work together, you might like to see what emerges in the responses and see if some of the questions should be revisited regularly (perhaps annually or every six months) as a way of reviewing the life of your small group or church as a discipleship community against the picture Luke offers us in Acts 2. Similarly, individuals could be invited to keep a journal to regularly reflect on their living of the holy habits.

In Acts 2:47, Luke says the believers enjoyed 'the goodwill of all the people', so there are also some creative ideas for ways in which your church or group could collectively practise the habit being explored in the local or wider community. These are thought-starter ideas, so be open to other ideas that emerge in your conversations.

You will also find some prayers and creative media ideas for this habit at the back of the book.

In all of this, keep your hearts and minds open to the Holy Spirit and be alert to the wonders of God's grace and the signs of God's love that emerge as, individually and collectively, you live this down-to-earth, holy way of life that Luke invites us to imitate.

Session outline

Session outline

One way your group time could be structured:

- **Opening prayer**
  (for example, the Holy Habits prayer on page 59)

- **Music moment**
  (see 'Listen', page 61)

- **Bible reading**

- **Reflection**

- **Discussion questions**

- Time for stories, testimonies or questions/issues that arise from the discussion

- Prayer

- **Ideas to do as a group**
  Spend a few minutes to agree when this will be carried out or to come up with other ideas

- Take-home questions/creative media ideas

- Closing prayer

| Steve Aisthorpe

Week 1

Freely you have received, freely give

Read Deuteronomy 15:7-10

If anyone is poor among your fellow Israelites in any of the towns of the land that the Lord your God is giving you, do not be hard-hearted or tight-fisted towards them. Rather, be open-handed and freely lend them whatever they need. Be careful not to harbour this wicked thought: 'The seventh year, the year for cancelling debts, is near,' so that you do not show ill will towards the needy among your fellow Israelites and give them nothing. They may then appeal to the Lord against you, and you will be found guilty of sin. Give generously to them and do so without a grudging heart; then because of this the Lord your God will bless you in all your work and in everything you put your hand to.   (NIV)

Reflection

'Ideas worth spreading'. This is the mantra of TED, an organisation conceived to enable leaders in the fields of technology, entertainment and design (hence 'TED') to come together and share ideas. Nowadays, the impact of TED talks is immense as every day millions of people hear important ideas delivered in a pithy and powerful format.

Moses wrestled with the same challenge identified by the founders of TED: how to ensure that messages of crucial significance would be understood. Deuteronomy was his answer. Here is powerful, persuasive instruction on how to live intentionally as God's people in response to his love and mercy.

It is a masterclass in communication. Nobody could hear this sermon and not be utterly convinced of the absolute necessity of cultivating a habit of extreme generosity. Today's passage begins and ends with positive and unequivocal instructions to foster practices of liberal lending and generous giving. In between is a warning about the peril of ignoring his urging.

Moses hammers home the importance of gladness and generosity, piling one adverb on to another to emphasise the attitude the Lord longs to see: *freely* lend; *generously* give. The meanness of a heart of stone and a tightly clenched fist is contrasted with the compassionate humanity of an open hand offered to those in need.

> O Lord, our provider, all we are and all we have come from you. Grant us the love and courage to live a life of big-heartedness and open-handedness. Amen

Questions

1 What does it mean to be poor or needy?

2 What kinds of situations tempt you to be hard-hearted or tight-fisted?

3 Have you experienced the blessing of being open-handed and/or have you had experiences that did not seem to go well?

4 How can we foster a culture of generosity in our church or community?

5 Are there guidelines or principles related to being open-handed or to freely lending that you have found helpful?

6 What might be 21st-century equivalents of 'Be careful not to harbour this wicked thought: "The seventh year, the year for cancelling debts, is near"'?

• • •

Idea to do as a group

> **1** How might you, individually or as a group, donate time to enhance the well-being of your community in ways that will not necessarily benefit you? Following the teaching of Jesus, whatever you decide to do, do it quietly and unobtrusively (Matthew 6:1–4). Take time to reflect on what you learned from this and how it might change your behaviour in the future.

Take-home questions

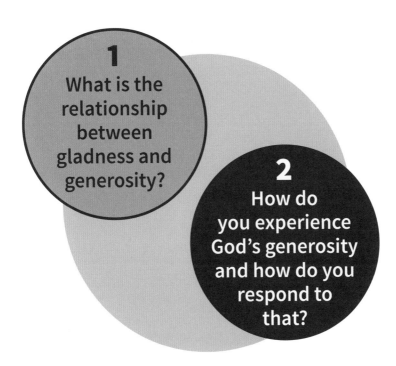

1
What is the relationship between gladness and generosity?

2
How do you experience God's generosity and how do you respond to that?

| Steve Aisthorpe

Week 2

The good shepherd

Read Psalm 23

The Lord is my shepherd, I lack nothing. He makes me lie down in green pastures, he leads me beside quiet waters, he refreshes my soul. He guides me along the right paths for his name's sake. Even though I walk through the darkest valley, I will fear no evil, for you are with me; your rod and your staff, they comfort me. You prepare a table before me in the presence of my enemies. You anoint my head with oil; my cup overflows. Surely your goodness and love will follow me all the days of my life, and I will dwell in the house of the Lord forever.   (NIV)

Reflection

A few years ago, after decades of excellent health, I plunged into a period of protracted illness. Like a roller coaster, swooping plunges into the depths were followed by painfully slow progress to regain previous levels, only to then be catapulted into the next gut-wrenching drop. Although I am normally an optimistic person, lengthy periods of chronic fatigue and lingering pain whittled away my resilience. During the deepest troughs, unable to read, there was a portion of scripture, one of the few I have managed to memorise, that brought encouragement and reassurance. This psalm was a well of assurance and an oasis of cheer while journeying through a desert of discouragement and despair.

The shepherds of David's world kept small flocks, harvesting wool over several years. They really did *lead* their sheep and they *knew* their sheep. A good shepherd enabled the flock to thrive by leading them to places of plentiful grazing, fresh water – and rest, untainted by fear of predators. David knew from experience the courage and commitment needed to be a good shepherd. He had killed bears and lions while protecting his father's sheep (1 Samuel 17:34–36). When Jesus said, 'I am the gate' (John 10:9), he had in mind the habit of the best shepherds to spend the night sleeping stretched across the entrance of the sheep fold, ensuring the safety and well-being of those under his charge in the most diligent and intimate way.

> Read again today's psalm, allowing the promises of provision, security, rest, guidance and hope to permeate the deepest parts of your being – and recognising the gladness that wells up in response.

Questions

1 Why do you think that Psalm 23 has become the best known of all the psalms?

2 Who can honestly say that they 'lack nothing'?

3 Where does the Lord lead you to refresh your soul?

4 How do you experience the guidance of the Lord?

5 In the context of the ancient Middle East, the phrase 'You anoint my head with oil; my cup overflows' speaks of generous hospitality. What might be the equivalent expression in our own day and culture?

6 What situations face your community, nation or the world which might be thought of as 'the darkest valley', and how might the Lord use his 'rod and staff' (which a shepherd uses to protect the flock from danger and draw them closer when they stray)?

• • •

Week 2

Idea to do as a group

1 For one month, whenever you consider buying something other than the essentials, rather than making the purchase, set aside a similar amount of money. At the end of the month, donate that amount to a person in need (anonymously) or a worthwhile cause. Keep a short journal of your experiences during this experiment with frugality and generosity. Share your experiences of your inner struggles and joys during this time (not the specifics, so as to avoid the pitfalls Jesus cautioned against in Matthew 6:1–4), what you learned and how it might change your behaviour in the future.

Take-home questions

1

In what aspects of life do you find it easy to be glad and generous, and in which areas is it more challenging? What support would be helpful?

2

For whom could you prepare a table of generosity?

| Jo Swinney

Week 3

Reclothed

Read Isaiah 61:1–3

The Spirit of the Sovereign Lord is on me, because the Lord has anointed me to proclaim good news to the poor. He has sent me to bind up the broken-hearted, to proclaim freedom for the captives and release from darkness for the prisoners, to proclaim the year of the Lord's favour and the day of vengeance of our God, to comfort all who mourn, and provide for those who grieve in Zion – to bestow on them a crown of beauty instead of ashes, the oil of joy instead of mourning, and a garment of praise instead of a spirit of despair. They will be called oaks of righteousness, a planting of the Lord for the display of his splendour.　(NIV)

Reflection

There is so much pain in the world. The poor, the broken-hearted, the captives and the prisoners, those who mourn and grieve, the despairing: they are everywhere. They are us.

How can we possibly be glad in the face of all that hurts, all that is unjust, all that takes our courage and tramples it in the cold, hard light of reality? What is this good news that will set us free?

Seven centuries after the prophet Isaiah delivered his hopeful message, a man stood up in a synagogue in the town of Nazareth and proclaimed that this scripture had been fulfilled in their hearing. You can read about it in Luke 4. Jesus Christ is God's comfort to a broken world. His life, death and resurrection give all of us reason for hope and a source of joy.

Our gladness in the face of all that is wrong is a 'display of his splendour' – a testament to the spiritual gift of joy in God through the Spirit. During the times our emotions register no joy, gladness becomes a discipline, a spiritual practice. We have to choose to wear the crown of beauty and the garment of praise.

> Whether or not it matches your mood today, put on the garment of praise. Worship the God who is the source of all joy and comfort.

Questions

1 What is the good news referred to at the beginning of this passage?

2 How was the life of Jesus a fulfilment of this passage?

3 Why does God choose the poor, the grieving and the prisoners through which to display his splendour?

4 What does it mean to put on 'a garment of praise'?

5 When have you chosen to praise God in the midst of a terrible situation?

6 What impact did it have on you and those around you?

• • •

Week 3

Idea to do as a group

1 Think about specific needs among those you know. Perhaps someone's washing machine has broken and they can't afford to replace it. Maybe you know a single mother who needs free babysitting or a pensioner who can't take care of their garden any longer. See how many of the items on the list you can tick off over the next week or two.

Take-home questions

1

In what ways does the practice of generosity increase our spiritual health?

2

In times of distress people often kindly say, 'Do let me know if there is anything I could do to help.' Might you need to ask for or receive some help at the moment? If so, let someone bless you with generosity.

| Jo Swinney

Week 4

Joyful generosity

Read Matthew 19:21–24

Jesus answered, 'If you want to be perfect, go, sell your possessions and give to the poor, and you will have treasure in heaven. Then come, follow me.' When the young man heard this, he went away sad, because he had great wealth. Then Jesus said to his disciples, 'Truly I tell you, it is hard for someone who is rich to enter the kingdom of heaven. Again I tell you, it is easier for a camel to go through the eye of a needle than for someone who is rich to enter the kingdom of God.'   (NIV)

Week 4

Reflection

Chuck Feeney is an Irish-American businessman who has made a fortune in duty-free shopping. He lives in a rented apartment, travels economy class and to date has given away over $8 billion. In a letter to fellow philanthropist Bill Gates, he explained, 'The process of – and most importantly, the results from – granting this wealth to good causes has been a rich source of joy and satisfaction to me and for my family.'

Humans have always been susceptible to idol worship – investing value and worth in inappropriate places. It is so easy to fall for the lie that possessions will make us happy, safe and powerful. That is why Jesus seems harsh and unreasonable in this exchange with the rich young man. How could anyone even consider giving everything away?

What Jesus knew, and what Chuck Feeney knows, is that radical generosity is the key that buys our freedom. There is real, true, priceless treasure in heaven. It is worth more than anything our grubby mitts can grasp on to. And it is ours for the taking once we stop hoarding and start giving.

> Lord God, I am sorry for undervaluing heavenly treasure and investing in the wrong kind of wealth. Help me to trust your judgement on what matters and to bless others with what I have. Amen

Questions

1 Jesus did not tell everyone he met to sell their possessions, but he did say it in this instance. What might explain his approach with this young man?

2 What do you think Jesus meant by 'treasure in heaven'?

3 Why is it so hard for the wealthy to enter the kingdom of God?

4 If you were the young man, what would you say to Jesus in response to his invitation to follow him?

5 Given that, in global and historical terms, all of us reading this book are fabulously wealthy (we can read, we have access to books), what can we do to avoid becoming slaves to our wealth?

6 On what basis do we enter the kingdom of God?

• • •

Idea to do as a group

1 Over the next few days, find as many ways as you can to be generous to strangers. This could mean paying the motorway toll for the car who comes after you, buying an extra coffee for the last person in the queue, carrying someone's shopping bags to their car or leaving a bar of chocolate on a random doorstep. Take note of how you feel after each occasion.

Take-home questions

1

What does it look like to embrace gladness as a discipline or holy habit?

2

In a private space reflect on what your heart's treasures are. Is there anything that limits your ability to respond to Jesus' call to follow him?

| David Spriggs

Week 5

Overflowing generosity

Read Luke 6:35–38

'But love your enemies, do good to them, and lend to them without expecting to get anything back. Then your reward will be great, and you will be children of the Most High, because he is kind to the ungrateful and wicked. Be merciful, just as your Father is merciful. Do not judge, and you will not be judged. Do not condemn, and you will not be condemned. Forgive, and you will be forgiven. Give, and it will be given to you. A good measure, pressed down, shaken together and running over, will be poured into your lap. For with the measure you use, it will be measured to you.' (NIV)

Week 5

Reflection

Generosity is the overflowing of God's heart. God's generosity is like a large waterfall. As the onrushing water reaches the waterfall's edge, it cascades and tumbles over. It falls and splashes anywhere and everywhere. It doesn't flow in an orderly straight line and through constructed channels. It's as though the water has been freed. Delighting in its freedom, it runs wild, bouncing and foaming as it hits rocks, splashing and spraying in every direction. Then, when the sun shines, a beautiful rainbow appears through the spray, celebrating its unfettered spirit. Such, says Jesus, is the generosity of God.

Over Christmas, I was given some bottles of good-quality grape juice – not just a couple of bottles but a box of twelve. Overflowing generosity! It was a heart-warming experience, all the more so because it was unexpected and unearned. This meant that I could be generous in return, giving some bottles to others and ensuring that our guests had ample supplies.

Jesus indicates several features of God's generosity. He gives without any expectation or impression that he expects to be paid back. He is kind. He is merciful, that is, he doesn't react to the damage people do by punishment or by withholding his generosity. He gives more than is necessary or expected. But if we want to experience this kind of generosity, then we also need to practise it.

> Think of times when you have been the recipient of other people's generosity. How did it make you feel towards them? How did it make you feel personally? When can you put this habit into practice?

Questions

1 'Generosity is the overflowing of God's heart.' Spend time in reflection, then share personal experiences of God's generosity and also times when you have seen this in church.

2 Such experiences often come through people God uses. How do you recognise these as 'from God'?

3 How do you discern God's generosity? Have you experienced a miracle of God's generosity?

4 How do such experiences make you feel towards God? How do you express your response? Do they lead you to greater freedom and generosity?

5 'Do not judge... Do not condemn.' Generosity is also about the habits of our heart. Do you judge rough sleepers, immigrants, refugees or those who have let you down? Where might you need to let God change your attitudes to others?

6 'Forgive, and you will be forgiven.' What can make it hard for us to forgive others? How can we help one another forgive?

• • •

Week 5

Idea to do as a group

1 Conduct a survey of 100 random houses around your church (two or three from around 40 streets). Put together five questions to enable them to tell you what help they would like from the church. Meet as a small group to pray about all their requests. Like Peter and John, many things you won't be able to respond to. But what is God calling you to offer to these people in the name of Jesus? Draw up a leaflet which lists three to five things you will do to meet people's requests and then revisit the 100 homes and either talk to people again or leave a leaflet. Don't be afraid to say that you don't have the resources for some ideas. Remember to explain what you can offer 'in the name of Jesus'. See what God does with your generosity! Get a group who will pray regularly for the next twelve months that God will cause people to praise him for 'what they see and hear'.

Take-home questions

1

Can you think of two factors which make it harder to continue to be generous and two which might help you grow in generosity?

2

How well does your church provide opportunities for those with less to make their contribution and to receive affirmation? Consider what could be done along these lines.

| David Spriggs

Week 6

Generosity spreading blessings far and wide

Read Luke 19:5–9

When Jesus reached the spot, he looked up and said to him, 'Zacchaeus, come down immediately. I must stay at your house today.' So he came down at once and welcomed him gladly. All the people saw this and began to mutter, 'He has gone to be the guest of a sinner.' But Zacchaeus stood up and said to the Lord, 'Look, Lord! Here and now I give half of my possessions to the poor, and if I have cheated anybody out of anything, I will pay back four times the amount.' Jesus said to him, 'Today salvation has come to this house, because this man, too, is a son of Abraham.'   (NIV)

Reflection

The prodigal's father showed his glad and generous heart by unexpectedly welcoming his son. Here, Zacchaeus' glad and generous heart is triggered when he is unexpectedly welcomed by Jesus. God's offer of unconditional love and unwarranted forgiveness has tremendous power to release in us the same qualities that we have received.

Hence Zacchaeus 'came down at once and welcomed him gladly'. Some people can feel almost as glad when the vicar remembers their name and speaks to them at the door; others, because they are surprised that they are allowed to come to church in jeans. For Zacchaeus, Jesus' offer to come to his house to eat with him blew him away.

There was nothing in the world that could have meant more to Zacchaeus. He did not need physical healing for himself or any family member; he did not have a theological question he needed solving by this brilliant young rabbi; he did not need feeding in a desert place. He needed to know God loved him. That's what Jesus' affirming words and actions conveyed.

It was not long before Zacchaeus' gladness transmuted into generosity. His experience of Jesus set him free: free to admit he had cheated others; free, too, to become Jericho's leading philanthropist.

This is one of the wonderful things about generosity – it can spread the blessing far and wide. There would be many households in Jericho that night who could afford wine and good food to celebrate because Zacchaeus was free to give.

> What steps will you take to express to others God's amazing love for you?

Questions

1 Jesus' words got to Zacchaeus' heart. Have you experienced such words personally? How can we learn to speak as Jesus did?

2 Can you think of instances where prejudice makes it hard for people to be generous?

3 Imagine together what the comments might have been when Zacchaeus announced that he was going to be generous. Share together any echoes of similar comments today in newspapers, social media and your church.

4 Discuss the impact on your community if your church announced that it would give half of all its assets to the poor. What might prevent you from being glad and generous in this way?

5 How does your church make deeply real and personal God's love for individuals? How could you celebrate this?

6 How can the group encourage each other to experience again the freeing love of Jesus? How can that love release you personally and as a community?

• • •

Week 6

Ideas to do as a group

1 Plan an event to which people bring whatever food, flowers or other appropriate gifts they can and then celebrate together. Consider whether to restrict this to the regular congregation or invite people around your church or your home. Ensure that there is a relaxed and happy atmosphere so that you can enjoy being glad and generous.

2 Select a couple of local charities which provide for those in need, maybe a food bank, a night shelter or a charity that provides Christmas gifts to families who are struggling. Set aside two months in the life of the church when each group and every individual is invited to celebrate God's love for them by giving to others, as Zacchaeus did. Then invite representatives from the chosen charities and present the gifts, explaining that God sets us free to give to others.

Take-home questions

1

How can stories of communities being glad and generous inspire you to better reflect the heart of God?

2

How would you or your church respond to overt and public expressions of emotion, whether vibrantly joyful, overtly exuberant or emotionally distressing (think again about John 12:3–8)?

3

What has caused you to be really joyful recently about the activities your church is involved in? Thank God for the joy of belonging to his family.

| David Gilmore

Week 7

Shaken and stirred

Read Acts 16:25–34 (abridged)

About midnight Paul and Silas were praying and singing hymns to God... Suddenly there was an earthquake, so violent that the foundations of the prison were shaken; and immediately all the doors were opened and everyone's chains were unfastened. When the jailer woke up and saw the prison doors wide open, he drew his sword and was about to kill himself.... But Paul shouted in a loud voice, 'Do not harm yourself, for we are all here.' The jailer called for lights, and rushing in, he fell down trembling before Paul and Silas. Then he brought them outside and said, 'Sirs, what must I do to be saved?' They answered, 'Believe on the Lord Jesus, and you will be saved, you and your household.' They spoke the world of the Lord to him and to all who were in his house. At the same hour of the night he took them and washed their wounds; then he and his entire family were baptised without delay. He brought them up into the house and set food before them; and he and his entire household rejoiced that he had become a believer in God.

(NRSV)

Reflection

I am a fan of James Bond movies. I grew up loving the fast cars, unbelievable gadgets and continual danger constantly surrounding Agent 007. I remember all the different Bond actors – one line they all have in common is when Bond orders his favourite libation: 'shaken not stirred'.

In our reading, the jailer has been shaken and stirred. The idea that he may have lost the prisoners has him so distraught that he sees suicide as his salvation. Yet, the one who has been jailed offers real hope, real salvation, to the jailer. This unbelievable act of generosity on the part of Paul leads to new life not only for the oppressor, but also for his family. How might our world be changed if we remembered to see *all* of God's family as just that... God's family? How might the 'chains' of addiction and abuse and heartache and loneliness and hopelessness be broken if we but offer a word of grace, believing that that word has the power to change any one and anything?

The glad sharing of the good news leads to a stirring transformation in the jailer, evidenced in his generous offering of medical treatment and food. But it goes much deeper! Paul and Silas' sharing leads to a glad response by the jailer and his entire household. Their generous spirits, despite their physical circumstances, lead to a transformation no one could have foreseen.

> Lord, shake and stir me to be an agent of your salvation.

Questions

1 What emotions come to mind when you think of being shaken and stirred?

2 Have you ever felt like you were about to lose everything? What did you do?

3 Has God ever shaken or stirred you? What did you do in response?

4 How, if ever, has your family been impacted by the Holy Spirit moving in you?

5 What might happen in your community (faith, family, neighbourhood) if you allowed the Holy Spirit to shake you up?

6 How might your answers to the previous questions affect your attitude to gladness and generosity?

● ● ●

Idea to do as a group

1 During a sermon when stewardship is emphasised, give each member in the congregation a £1 coin with instructions to find an imaginative way to give their gift in such a way as to bless someone else's life. For example, the gift might be used at the local coffee shop to pay for a person in the queue. This gift is to be given without fanfare or announcement on the part of the giver.

The next Sunday (or regular time of gathering), set aside time during the worship for people to share what, where, how and why they gave of their free gift.

Were they more glad giving from their abundance or from nothing? How might their act(s) of glad giving affect the lives of those who received the unasked-for gift?

Take-home questions

1
How might the lives of those in your community be positively affected if your words, actions and attitudes displayed a gladness in your giving?

2
Reflect on the hymns and worship songs you sing and the promises regarding generosity that you make in singing them. Are there any promises that need to be lived out more fully?

| David Gilmore

Week 8

Giving until it feels good

Read 2 Corinthians 9:6–11

The point is this: the one who sows sparingly will also reap sparingly, and the one who sows bountifully will also reap bountifully. Each of you must give as you have made up your mind, not reluctantly or under compulsion, for God loves a cheerful giver. And God is able to provide you with every blessing in abundance, so that by always having enough of everything, you may share abundantly in every good work. As it is written, 'He scatters abroad, he gives to the poor; his righteousness endures forever.' He who supplies seed to the sower and bread for food will supply and multiply your seed for sowing and increase the harvest of your righteousness. You will be enriched in every way for your great generosity, which will produce thanksgiving to God through us.   (NRSV)

Reflection

Growing up in a Christian home in the US, I was taught at an early age that when the offering plate was passed around, I was supposed to put something in it. In fact, my grandmother would give me a nickel or dime to place in it. Now that I'm an adult, I can admit that I wanted to use my nickel or dime to buy candy. Later, I wanted to use my money in the clothing store or movie theatre rather than place it in an offering plate. You see, I didn't understand the significance of, or the theology in, my giving.

It was not until I had fallen away and then found my way back to church that I began to study the *why* behind giving. I don't give because of what I may receive in turn. This is not a quid pro quo relationship between the Lord and me, where I'm mistaking God for a cash machine, dating service or fortune teller. No, my giving is done with genuine gladness, because I'm reminded in these acts of what Christ gave for me. My giving is done with deep gratitude, because I know Jesus gave his all for me. There is no compunction or reticence in my giving, because the Lord has provided more than I could have imagined or deserved!

When I was a local church pastor, there was a rather cantankerous older gentleman who loudly asked me, 'Do you want to see me or my money?' I explained that I wanted to see both, but for different reasons. I wanted to see the man, because this was the means for us to enter into an authentic, trusting, loving relationship. I also wanted to see him giving, because this is an act of worship, or an encounter with the divine, where an authentic, trusting, loving relationship is being offered.

> How good do you feel when called to give? Remembering the sacrificial gift of Jesus should make us feel really good and grateful and generous in our giving.

Questions

1 Who or what taught you to give?

2 What, if any, is the motivation behind your giving (e.g. self-satisfaction or desire to please God)?

3 Do you see giving as an act of worship or charity? Is there a difference?

4 Do you limit your giving to Sunday mornings in worship?

5 What reason(s) do you have to be cheerful? Does it translate to your giving?

6 What or who has God given you as a gift? How do you treat it or them?

Week 8

Idea to do as a group

1 During winter, have a group of church members serve soup or stew at a public park where homeless people are known to frequent. Each member is to contribute at least one ingredient to the soup and, if capable, take turns stirring the pot. Everyone should also participate in setting up the tables, food and utensils. Additionally, each member should participate in serving the food and interacting with the 'least, last and lost' of the community.

After this act of generosity is completed, have a discussion with the church members, asking them to share their experiences and how it has affected them. Was there gladness in their giving?

Take-home questions

1
What gifts bring you gladness and make you want to give abundantly or generously?

2
How might glad and generous giving become more meaningful in your life and in the lives of your family?

For your notes

For your notes

Prayers

The Holy Habits prayer

Endurance produces character, and character produces hope,
and hope does not disappoint us...
Gracious and ever-loving God, we offer our lives to you.
Help us always to be open to your Spirit in our thoughts
and feelings and actions.
Support us as we seek to learn more about those habits of
the Christian life
which, as we practise them, will form in us the character
of Jesus
by establishing us in the way of faith, hope and love.
Amen

A collect

Most gracious God, all good things come from you and are
signs of your love.
May our gratitude fill us with gladness, and our gladness
with generosity,
that we may express our joy in the service of others,
and give in thankfulness for what we have received,
through Jesus Christ our Lord.
Amen

Prayers

A prayer of giving thanks

This is the day, Lord,
this is the day we come to worship together.
We come because we are amazed at your generosity,
amazed at so much beauty,
so much love,
so much care offered to each and all who are open,
open to being part of your wondrous kingdom,
open to living lives of beauty and love and care.

How can we thank you for your gracious invitation?
Thank you for the joy in our lives,
for the kindness shown, even by strangers,
the moments when we have entertained angels
and not recognised them until they have left
and left us the better for their companionship.

We thank you in the everyday,
in the offered hand,
the encouraging word,
the touch of friendship.

This is the day, Lord,
each day in your presence is a day of gladness
and so we worship you, this day and always.
Amen

Creative media ideas

Watch

Pollyanna (U, 1960, 2h14m)

A young girl, Pollyanna (played by Hayley Mills in this classic movie), moves to live with her embittered aunt in the early 1900s. She introduces her aunt, and the rest of the town, to her 'glad game', and shows her determination to see the best in life. She soon turns around the attitude of the town, who in turn help her to see the good in life when tragedy happens. Based on a book of the same name by Eleanor H. Porter.

- Being described as 'Pollyanna-ish' is often a criticism of someone who is overly positive and doesn't live in the real world. In the film, what does Pollyanna bring that is wholesome and healing to others' lives? Is she unrealistic, or just hopeful about other people? How is she a gift to others?

Read

'Thanksgiving' by Malcolm Guite

Find this poem online. What does it say to you about gladness and generosity?

Listen

'Happy' by Pharrell Williams

Whole-church resources

Individual copy £4.99

Holy Habits is an adventure in Christian discipleship. Inspired by Luke's model of church found in Acts 2:42–47, it identifies ten habits and encourages the development of a way of life formed by them. These resources are designed to help churches explore the habits creatively in a range of contexts and live them out in whole-life, intergenerational, missional discipleship.

MISSIONAL DISCIPLESHIP RESOURCES FOR CHURCHES

HOLYHABITS

Original design by morsebrowndesign.co.uk & penguinboy.net

These new additions to the Holy Habits resources have been developed to help churches and individuals explore the Holy Habits through prayerful engagement with the Bible and live them out in whole-life, missional discipleship.

Bible Reflections   Edited by Andrew Roberts | Individual copy £3.99

Each set of Bible reading notes contains eight weeks of devotional material. Four writers bring different perspectives on the habit in question through their reflections on passages drawn from across the Bible narrative.

Group Studies   Edited by Andrew Roberts | Individual copy £6.99

Each leader's guide contains eight sessions of Bible study material, providing off-the-peg material to help churches get started or continue with Holy Habits. Each session includes a Bible passage, reflections, group questions, community/outreach ideas, art and media links and a prayer.

Find out more at holyhabits.org.uk
and brfonline.org.uk/collections/holy-habits
Download a leaflet for your church leadership at
brfonline.org.uk/holyhabitsdownload

Praise for the original Holy Habits resources

'Here are some varied and rich resources to help further deepen our discipleship of Christ, encouraging and enabling us to adopt the life-transforming habits that make for following Jesus.'
Revd Dr Martyn Atkins, Team Leader & Superintendent Minister, Methodist Central Hall, Westminster

'The Holy Habits resources will help you, your church, your fellowship group, to engage in a journey of discovery about what it really means to be a disciple today. I know you will be encouraged, challenged and inspired as you read and work your way through… There is lots to study together and pray about, and that can only be good as our churches today seek to bring about the kingdom of God.'
Revd Loraine Mellor, President of the Methodist Conference 2017/18

'The Holy Habits resources help weave the spiritual through everyday life. They're a great tool that just get better with use. They help us grow in our desire to follow Jesus as their concern is formation not simply information.'
Olive Fleming Drane and John Drane

'The Holy Habits resources are an insightful and comprehensive manual for living in the way of Jesus in the 21st century: an imaginative, faithful and practical gift for the church that will sustain and invigorate our life and mission in a demanding world. The Holy Habits resources are potentially transformational for a church.'
Revd Ian Adams, Mission Spirituality Adviser for Church Mission Society

'To understand the disciplines of the Christian life without practising them habitually is like owning a fine collection of soap but never having a wash. The team behind Holy Habits knows this, which is why they have produced these excellent and practical resources. Use them, and by God's grace you will grow in holiness.'
Paul Bayes, Bishop of Liverpool